"THE FREE MARKET doesn't work as the basic mechanism for providing education," declared Diane Ravitch, former assistant secretary of education under George H. W. Bush and current teachers union darling.

This disdain for markets among the education establishment is the major obstacle facing efforts to reform America's K-12 education system. Contrary to the claims of opponents, expanding choice via vouchers, charters, and tax credits would make our schools significantly better. Market forces have enabled improvements in almost all aspects of our life, and they can do the same in education.

There are, however, very few market forces currently operating in our K-12 education system. We primarily assign students to schools based on where they live. We provide ever-increasing funds to public schools regardless of how well students learn, nearly tripling real expenditures over the past four decades to more than $600 billion per year. It is virtually impossible to fire a teacher for poor performance. In general, schools do not have to compete on price or quality to continue operating and employing all of their staff.

No business looks like this. Even relatively few government services are provided the same way as those in K-12 education. We do not assign senior citizens to hospitals or to doctors in their neighborhoods in order to receive Medicare benefits. We do not compel retirees to live in government-operated nursing homes to obtain housing with Social Security benefits. While food stamps place some restrictions on what items *can* be purchased, the program does not compel recipients to receive their food at government-operated soup kitchens or grocery stores.

In short, choice and competition are the norm in public and private enterprises. It should be noted that none of these markets – public or private – is completely "free."

All markets are subject to some amount of government regulation. The question is not whether we should have "free markets" in education; the question is why we have embraced regulated markets in almost all domains of our lives, but not in K-12 education.

Even within education, we have remarkably robust markets with large government subsidies, as long as the students are not between the ages of 6 and 17. For students below the age of 6, we offer a credit on federal income taxes to assist parents in paying tuition at the preschool of their choice: public or private, religious or secular. After the age of 17, we offer students Pell grants, Stafford loans, and Hope scholarships to assist them in attending the college of their choice.

Why then does Diane Ravitch and the rest of the education establishment assert that markets don't work in K-12 education? Is K-12 education so unusual that it has to be arranged differently from almost every other private, public, and even educational system? No. The reality is that the K-12 establishment's hostility to markets is fueled by raw self-interest disguised as benevolent paternalism. There are more than 6.3 million people currently employed by public schools, of whom 3.2 million are teachers. And the teachers unions boast 4.7 million members (3.2 million for the National Education Association and 1.5 million for the American Federation of Teachers). The power of these unions as well as the jobs, compensation, and worldview of their members are intertwined with the current nonmarket method of delivering education. Given that there are fewer than 113 million full-time workers in the U.S., these 6.3 million public school employees constitute what Abraham Lincoln might have called a "peculiar and powerful interest," significantly distorting the design of our education system.

Of course, the education establishment does not admit to themselves or to others that they are putting the interests of adults ahead of the education of children. On the

*Choice and competition are
the norm in public and
private enterprises.*

contrary, they have developed an elaborate
set of rationalizations for their opposition to
expanded markets in k-12 education, which
most of them believe with complete sincerity.
Their self-interest encourages self-delusion.

The purpose of this Broadside is to consider and rebut the major objections that
are raised to expanding choice and competition in education. But let me emphasize
at the outset that the burden of proof should
not be on the supporters of expanded choice.
On the contrary, the burden should be
on the opponents of expanded choice and
competition. Why is it that education should
fail to benefit from the tonic of expanded
choice and market freedom? In virtually
every other human activity, competition

and freedom of choice act as stimulants to achievement. Why should education be the sole exception? Having choice and competition is the *normal* arrangement, while the current design of K-12 education is highly *abnormal.* Sustaining something so unusual requires exceptional justification.

Let us review the justifications that are typically offered for opposing market reforms of the abnormal design of K-12 education.

CANARD 1: CHOICE IS NOT A PANACEA

One way in which opponents undercut expanded choice and competition is by establishing an unreasonably high bar for success. If choice has not "transformed" a failing school system, produced a "miracle," or lived up to the most extravagant prediction that any supporter ever made, then it must be a failure. Stanford University professor Martin Carnoy dismisses vouchers with this type of argument, writing, "Even if limited studies do show marginal gains by some students, vouchers are clearly not a cure-all." Or, as Diane Ravitch put it, "We now know that choice is no panacea."

Even some people predisposed to support choice have begun repeating this line. Sol Stern, writing about the Milwaukee voucher program in the Manhattan Institute's *City Journal*, despaired, "Fifteen years into the most expansive school choice program tried in any urban school district [and] no 'Milwaukee miracle,' no transformation of

---

Why is it that education should fail to benefit from the tonic of expanded choice and market freedom?

---

the public schools, has taken place." The Fordham Institute's Chester Finn expressed "growing sympathy" for this disappointment, concluding that we have had "too much trust in market forces."

The reality is that we've had very small expansions in the use of market forces, so, not surprisingly, we've had modest effects from choice programs. Programs tend to include relatively few students. Prior to the start of the current round of state legislative sessions, there were 26 voucher or tax-credit scholarship programs, none of which served more than 25,000 students. In aggregate, these private school choice programs served fewer than 200,000 of the nation's nearly 55 million school-age children, a mere fraction of 1 percent.

In addition, traditional public school systems are often partially or entirely held harmless against the financial repercussions of losing students to choice programs. If a business were partially or entirely compensated for the customers it lost, we wouldn't expect it to change dramatically to attract or retain customers. This is exactly how Frederick Hess of the American Enterprise

Institute sees the situation in Milwaukee: "Perhaps the lack of response should not be surprising, as MPS [Milwaukee Public Schools] has been largely unscathed by 'competition.' The district's enrollment has remained stable; it was ninety-two thousand in 1990 and ninety-one thousand last year. Over the same period, MPS boosted per-pupil spending by more than 90 percent (from $6,200 to more than $12,100) and increased the teacher workforce by more than 20 percent."

In general, those administering traditional school systems believe their schools cannot be closed or experience significant job losses even if they lose a large number of students to competitors. Their confidence in their political resources to counteract competitive threats has muted their educational response.

Even charter schools, with more than 1.7 million students, pose a limited competitive threat to traditional public school systems. First, charter schools have to receive permission to operate from an authority that is often closely connected to traditional public schools. These charter authorizers often favor granting charters to schools that tend to be less of a competitive threat, such as charter schools for dropouts, adjudicated youth, and other groups that traditional public schools don't mind losing. Second, charter schools are subject to considerable government regulation, which limits their ability to be operationally distinct from traditional public schools. And third, charter schools tend to receive significantly less per-pupil funding than traditional schools do, which partially holds the traditional system financially harmless and limits the scope and quality of their potential charter competitors.

The point is that choice has not yet had a more profound effect, because choice so far has been very limited. But we can change that. If we adopt significantly expanded choice programs that are designed to produce competitive responses, we should see choice make a much bigger difference. In particular, we would have to design programs so they would not hold traditional public schools harmless from the financial repercussions of losing students. And we would have to convince traditional public schools – and the voters who fund them – that we can no longer afford to protect school systems and jobs in schools that are unable to attract and retain students. I am not saying that these are easy things to accomplish. They are not. But we are already seeing them occur bit by bit as the failure of traditional public schools becomes ever more glaring and new, larger, and better-designed programs fostering school choice are being adopted.

Making competition through choice meaningful may not produce miracle cures, but, then again, nothing else does either. None of the reforms favored by the education establishment, such as spending more money, lowering class size, revising curricula, imposing standards, or altering teaching techniques, have produced significant improvements, let alone miracles. What is needed are not miracles or panaceas but real-world improvements in educational performance. By holding school choice to an impossibly high standard, partisans of the entrenched educational establishment stifle genuine educational reform while covertly protecting their perquisites and immunity from competition. Miracles shouldn't be the standard by which educational programs are judged.

Canard 2: There Is No Evidence that Students in Choice Programs Have Higher Achievement

Expanding school choice has not miraculously transformed public school systems, but there is very strong evidence that it has benefited the students who are offered additional options. When looking at research on how choice has affected students who get to choose – or what are called "participant effects" – it is important to focus on the highest-quality studies in which students are randomly assigned to being offered a voucher or returning to traditional public schools. These studies are like the ones used in medical research, in which subjects are assigned by lottery to treatment and control groups. On average, the two groups are identical except for whether they get the treatment or not, so any observed outcome can be attributed to that treatment and not to some pre-existing difference.

We can no longer afford to protect school systems and jobs in schools that are unable to attract and retain students.

The reason it is essential to focus on random-assignment studies in education is that we know student backgrounds have a very strong influence on their outcomes. If we don't assign students to be offered choices by lottery, we cannot be sure that we've separated the influence of those background factors from the effects of receiving choice. Random assignment is the gold standard in education research. It is the only way to ensure an apple-to-apple comparison and should be favored whenever available.

Happily, there are nine random-assignment studies of participant effects that present 10 analyses of voucher experiments. All of them have been peer-reviewed and published – and all but one show significant positive results.

Six analyses find significant overall improvements in academic outcomes when students are offered vouchers: Cowen, *Policy Studies Journal*, 2008; Greene, *Education Matters*, 2001; Greene, Peterson, and Du, *Education and Urban Society*, 1999; Howell, et al., *Journal of Policy Analysis and Management*, 2002 (Washington, D.C., results); Rouse; *Quarterly Journal of Economics*, 1998; and Wolf, et al., U.S. Department of Education, 2010.

Three analyses find significant benefits for at least one important subgroup of participants, like African-American students: Barnard, et al., *Journal of the American Statistical Association*, 2003; Howell, et al., *Journal of Policy Analysis and Management*, 2002 (Dayton, Ohio, results); and Peterson and Howell, *American Behavioral Scientist*, 2004.

These analyses report the results of voucher experiments in Charlotte, Dayton, Milwaukee, New York City, and Washington, D.C. We have multiple teams of researchers independently confirming the positive results from multiple experiments. Some analyses find that vouchers improve student achievement on standardized tests in either math or reading, while others find improvements in both subjects. Some analyses find that the benefits occur only for African-American or low-income students, while others find that the benefits occur for all students examined. The Wolf et al. analysis reports that vouchers in Washington, D.C., significantly increased the probability that students would graduate from high school in addition to improving their standardized test scores. Impressively, all nine of these analyses find positive results.

One random-assignment study (Krueger and Zhu, *American Behavioral Scientist*, 2004) reanalyzed Peterson and Howell's examination of the New York voucher experiment and found null results if students without baseline testing were included in the analysis and if a nonconventional definition of student race was employed. The point is that even after making some questionable decisions, the worst that Krueger and Zhu could find was that vouchers made no difference.

I am not aware of any other educational policy that has been the subject of 10 published random-assignment analyses. Indeed, most educational policies have never been examined by a *single* random-assignment study. And yet despite this impressive collection of random-assignment research that overwhelmingly finds positive effects, the American Federation of Teachers still declares that "research shows that vouchers don't improve outcomes for kids who receive them." The National Education Association concurs: "There is no evidence that vouchers improve student learning. Every serious study of voucher plans has concluded that vouchers do not improve student achievement."

Asking the teachers unions about what voucher research shows is a bit like asking the Tobacco Institute about the research on smoking and cancer or the sugar lobby about the merits of corn syrup. If we focus on gold-standard research, which not all reviews do (see, for example, Rouse and Barrow, *Annual Review of Economics*, 2009), the evidence clearly shows that students do better academically when their choices are expanded to include private schools.

Even charter schools, which are weak tea as far as choice is concerned, benefit students who attend them. Again, focusing only on random assignment, there are four studies, all of which find significant benefits for at least some types of students: Abdulkadiroglu, et al., *Quarterly Journal of Economics*, 2011; Gleason, et al., U.S. Department of Education, 2010;

Hoxby and Rockoff, *Education Next*, 2005; and Hoxby, et al., National Bureau of Economic Research, 2009.

The Gleason et al. study only finds benefits for urban students. This is consistent with the positive results observed from the others, which examined charter schools in Boston, Chicago, and New York City. Interestingly, the Abdulkadiroglu et al. random-assignment study of charter schools in Boston fails to find any benefit for students attending charter schools operated under union rules. The extent to which choice improves outcomes may be related to how different charters are really allowed to be.

There is also an often-mentioned charter evaluation by Margaret Raymond of Stanford University, which finds mixed results for charter schools nationwide. But it is important to note that this study is not based on random assignment. Instead, it attempts to match students on observed characteristics. Of course, the students who choose to attend

> *Asking the teachers unions about what voucher research shows is a bit like asking the Tobacco Institute about the research on smoking and cancer.*

a charter school differ significantly on at least one unobserved characteristic: the one that motivated them to apply to a charter school. This difference can bias the results. And since charter schools tend to be geared toward disadvantaged populations, the direction of that bias may well suppress positive charter effects.

A comprehensive review of all random-assignment voucher and charter studies provides convincing evidence for a conclusion that we normally take for granted: People tend to do better when they have more choices. What is true in other areas of life is also true in education. Choice and competition enhance performance.

CANARD 3: CHOICE HURTS STUDENTS WHO REMAIN IN TRADITIONAL PUBLIC SCHOOLS

As I mentioned above, choice programs are not currently large enough or strong enough to "transform" traditional public systems. Nevertheless, we still have a rigorous body of research that has been able to detect modest positive reactions to even the limited expansions in choice and competition that have been adopted.

When the question is how choice affects public schools, however, we do not have any random-assignment studies to consider. It simply isn't practical to randomly assign entire public school systems to face increased competition. Instead, researchers have to identify small variations in the amount of competition that public schools face within the same system.

Typically, researchers use "density" or "proximity" measures to gauge these small variations in competition. Density measures involve counting the number of voucher or charter competitors within a given radius of each traditional public school. If there are more voucher or charter schools within a 5- or 10-mile radius, we assume that the traditional public school faces greater competitive pressure. Alternatively, proximity measures focus on the distance between a traditional public school and the closest voucher or charter school. The closer the competitor, the more competition a school is thought to face.

Both density and proximity measures are highly imperfect proxies for competition. They are based on the assumption that transportation costs are high, so families are much less likely to choose a school farther away. In addition, density and proximity measures assume that all schools are competing for all students and that the market is not segmented so that some schools near each other may be seeking completely different kinds of students.

Imagine if we tried to use density or proximity measures to gauge the effect that competition among restaurants in Manhattan has on their quality. We would count the number of "competitors" within a certain radius of each restaurant (or measure the distance to the closest competitor) and then see if our proxy for competition could predict the restaurant quality, using something like a Zagat rating as an indicator of quality.

I'm confident that we would find little relationship between restaurant density or proximity in Manhattan and the quality of restaurants. As it turns out, transportation costs are not very high within a highly dense city with extensive public transportation, so going another mile on the subway to a restaurant is trivial. In addition, the restaurant market is segmented. A fancy

French restaurant may be located next to a McDonald's, but that doesn't mean they are competing for the same customers.

If researchers used the same methods to examine the effect of restaurant competition on quality that they use for school competition, they could easily come to the conclusion that competition has no effect on the quality of restaurants. They might suggest that restaurateurs don't do it for the money; they do it because they care about food. Of course, no one would believe this. Almost everyone believes that competition among restaurants (or any kind of organization) tends to improve quality and constrain costs. We recognize that people can also be motivated by caring about their craft, but competition helps attract people to work on the things they care about and pushes them to be better at it.

Searching for evidence that competition has this motivational effect in each industry is like testing for gravity in each room of your house. Once we've established the general principle, little is to be gained by continually seeking to confirm it in every particular application. In addition, if we have imperfect measures and constrained experiments, we could easily fail to observe something that we think is generally true. If I drop a bowling ball in each room of my house to test that gravity works the same everywhere, I may not find that the ball always falls to the floor. Sometimes there will be a bed or sofa in the way. That doesn't disprove gravity; it just shows that sometimes there are obstacles that prevent gravity from producing the result we expected.

The K-12 education system is filled with obstacles that could prevent modest expansions of competition from producing the effects we would normally expect from competition. Public school systems have political resources to help hold them harmless against the loss of students to competitors. That doesn't mean we should give up on harnessing the power of competition to improve schools. That just means that we have to work on designing educational markets so that competition can be allowed to produce its benefits.

The amazing thing is that despite all of these obstacles to confirming that competition works in education as it does everywhere else, we still see strong evidence that traditional public schools react constructively to competitive pressure. Introduce competition, and student achievement improves. Greg Forster of the Foundation for Educational Choice reviewed the evidence on competitive effects of private school choice on traditional public schools. He identified 19 studies that directly addressed the question. All but one of those studies observed a significant improvement in academic achievement by students at traditional public schools in response to expanded choice and competition.

You'll probably be amused to learn that the one study that failed to find any effect, positive or negative, was co-authored by me. In that study, Marcus Winters and I examined the competitive response by Washington, D.C., public schools to increased competition from the voucher program in that city. Importantly, that program was designed so that D.C. public schools would not lose any money if they lost students. In fact, Congress gave the D.C. public system a significant increase in funding to sweeten the bitter pill of having to accept the voucher program. It is hardly surprising that when schools are given more money and jobs even when they lose students, they tend not to respond to competition.

But private school choice programs in other locations, including Milwaukee, Florida, Ohio, San Antonio, Maine, and Vermont, placed at least some public school funding in jeopardy. And in those places, researchers were able to detect positive competitive responses. The improvements were generally modest. None of these public school systems was miraculously transformed. But the fact that we observe any response from limited programs with imperfect measures helps confirm that gravity also works in public schools.

If you don't find Greg Forster's review of the literature convincing because he writes for a choice advocacy group, and if you still need proof that gravity operates in public schools, let me suggest another review of research on competition in education conducted by

---

Attending private or charter schools helps (or at least does not hurt) students in being more tolerant of the political activities of people from groups they strongly dislike.

Clive Belfield and Henry Levin of Teachers College at Columbia University. Belfield and Levin are hardly choice enthusiasts, nor is Teachers College a pro-voucher advocacy organization. Their review focuses on studies of competition among public school districts rather than on competition from private school choice programs. They write, "The sampling strategy identified more than 41 relevant empirical studies. A sizable majority report beneficial effects of competition, and many report statistically significant correlations. For each study, the effect size of an increase of competition by one standard deviation is reported. The positive gains from competition are modest in scope with respect to realistic changes in levels of competition."

Given our strong theoretical expectations that competition should motivate public school improvement and a breadth of evidence that it does so, it is frustrating that people such as the writers of the *New York Times* editorial page declare, "Vouchers do nothing to improve education for those remaining in the public system. In theory, they are supposed to cause bad schools to reform themselves by threatening them with market competition. In fact, they make reform harder, if not impossible, by siphoning away meager resources and skimming off good students, leaving the most troubled children and the most apathetic families behind."

But there are no "facts" to be found in this *New York Times* editorial or in any of the other similar denunciations of school choice for hurting traditional public schools. Instead, all they have is an odd theory that public schools are hurt if they have to compete for funds. In virtually no other aspect of their life would these people believe that the best way to ensure quality is to guarantee organizations ever-increasing resources regardless of performance and with no prospect of having to compete. In this one room, they believe antigravity works.

Canard 4: Choice Segregates

Kweisi Mfume, the former president of the NAACP, put it succinctly: "Vouchers don't educate, they segregate." Opponents of choice need more than rhyming to make a convincing argument that choice segregates. They need a sensible definition of segregation. They also need evidence that allowing students to choose schools produces more segregation than the currently prevalent system of assigning students to schools based on where they live. Choice opponents have neither of these.

A sensible definition of segregation would feature the *involuntary* separation of groups of people. Choice, by definition, is voluntary. If families chose the school that their children attended, whatever its racial composition, it would seem impossible to describe that school as segregated. If families were so constrained that they did not really have choices, then we could still conceive of segregation in a choice system – but it would be a phony choice system. The antidote to that problem, however, would be to make families' choices real by offering them more options, not fewer.

The distinction between voluntary and involuntary separation of groups of people is noticeably absent in much of the most influential – and inflammatory – writing on the topic. For example, the Civil Rights Project, headed by Gary Orfield, issued a report that concluded, "More than two-fifths of black charter school students attended 'apartheid' schools, where 99% of students were from underrepresented minority backgrounds." Let's leave aside how a group that constitutes 99 percent of an organization could be "underrepresented," since this is typical of the fuzzy thinking in this literature. Instead, let's focus on the inflammatory use of the word "apartheid" to describe the racially homogenous schools that some black families voluntarily choose. This would be like calling

---

Part of the appeal of school choice is that it allows families to find schools that work best given their particular situation.

Jewish day schools that Jewish families voluntarily choose "concentration camp" schools. Equating terms that describe violent government repression that is completely involuntary in nature with the voluntary choices of individuals is highly irresponsible and misleading.

Opponents of school choice would be on (somewhat) stronger ground if they avoided these hyperbolic terms and shifted their claim to "stratification" instead of "segregation." The National Education Association does this when they allege, "A pure voucher system would only encourage economic, racial, ethnic, and religious stratification in our society." It is unclear under what circumstances, if any, we find voluntary "stratification" objectionable, but at least this defines the issue correctly.

Even assuming that "stratification" is problematic, the empirical evidence suggests that expanding choice tends to *reduce* stratification, not increase it. Remember that under the status quo system, we assign most students to schools based on where they live.

When we deviate from strict catchment zones, we rarely permit students to attend schools outside their school district other than through voucher and charter programs. Constraining students to attend schools within their politically drawn catchment and district boundaries tends to reproduce and reinforce racially stratified patterns in housing. Some people find that stratification in housing bothersome, but almost no one advocates assigning families to homes to reduce it.

Besides, by allowing students to choose schools outside their neighborhood or district, choice should lessen the severity of stratification by race. Duke University economist Thomas Nechyba has published a series of articles that find integration advantages in detaching schooling from housing through school choice: "[P]rivate school vouchers can further lessen residential income segregation and ... these segregation results are robust to alternative assumptions about school competition." In addition, I have compared the extent of racial mixing in public and private school lunchrooms, classrooms, and in the aftermath of adopting voucher programs. In general, the empirical evidence confirms that choice reduces stratification by allowing students to attend schools outside their racially homogenous neighborhoods.

Greg Forster reviewed the research on the effect of private school choice on stratification for the Foundation for Educational Choice. In the 10 studies he identified as employing an acceptable methodology, he found that they all consistently showed reductions in stratification in private school settings relative to traditional public schools. And if we consider efforts by traditional public schools to reduce segregation, virtually all of them involve using choice, like magnet schools, to improve the mixing of students from different backgrounds in the same school. If traditional public schools and courts think that choice is a tool that reduces stratification, it is not clear why we should think otherwise when it comes to expanding choice with vouchers or charters.

CANARD 5: CHOICE UNDERMINES CIVIC VALUES

Schools don't just teach academic subjects. They are also supposed to teach students how to be effective citizens. It has been widely believed that government-operated schools have an important advantage when it comes to instilling civic virtues and, further, that expanding school choice might undermine those virtues. Rutgers political theorist Benjamin Barber captures this view: "Public schools are not merely schools for the public, but schools of publicness: institutions where we learn what it means to be a public and start down the road toward common national and civic identity. They are the forges of our citizenship and the bedrock of our democracy."

These are flowery words, but do they reflect reality? Are private schools, in general, any less committed to or effective at conveying the basic tools of good citizenship? Simply having the word "public" in public schools does not make them serve public ends more effectively. Ultimately, this is an empirical question, not a linguistic one.

My colleague Patrick Wolf of the University of Arkansas conducted a comprehensive review of the research literature on this issue. He identified 21 studies that examined the effects of choice on seven civic outcomes for students: political tolerance, volunteerism, political knowledge, political

---

The safest and best way to get quality curriculum, assessments, and pedagogy is to decentralize power through choice.

---

participation, social capital, civic skills, and patriotism. Some studies presented results on more than one of these outcomes so that, in total, there were 59 analyses. All but three of these 59 analyses showed that choice schools did as well or better than traditional public schools at producing desired civic values. Thirty-three analyses showed that choice schools significantly outperformed traditional public schools.

To make these analyses more concrete, let's focus on the research about political tolerance. Political scientists have developed a methodology for measuring tolerance in which they ask subjects to identify their least-liked groups. They then ask subjects how willing they would be to let members of that group engage in political activities, such as running for elected office, holding a rally, or having the local library carry their books. The more willing people are to let members of their least-liked group engage in these political activities, the more tolerant they are considered to be. Among the 13 rigorous analyses of this issue, five showed an advantage for choice schools, and eight showed no difference. In general, it appears that attending private or charter schools helps (or at least does not hurt) students in being more tolerant of the political activities of people from groups they strongly dislike.

It is unclear why choice schools tend to produce better civic outcomes. It is possible that the advantage private schools have in teaching reading and math extends to civic issues as well. It is also possible that public schools have been hog-tied by political correctness, which hinders their ability to have the kind of open and honest conversations that effectively convey desired political values. Maybe the act of exercising their own freedom through choice makes students more aware of the freedoms of others. Whatever the explanation, the evidence clearly shows that civic concerns are no reason to oppose the expansion of school choice and competition.

* * *

Canard 6: Choice Is a Distraction from More-Productive Reforms

"We know what works," defenders of the education establishment like to say. "Just give us the resources to do it." Choice, according to this argument, is just a distraction from these other proven reforms.

First, it is important to note that real per-pupil expenditures over the past four decades have more than doubled, and yet achievement for 17-year-olds on the National Assessment of Educational Progress and high school graduation rates have remained virtually unchanged over this period. If we just needed the resources to do what worked, we should have seen it work by now.

Second, it is not at all obvious that we know what "works." We certainly don't know what works for all students in all circumstances, since kids are so varied in their needs and abilities. Part of the appeal of school choice is that it allows families to find schools that work best given their particular situation.

Traditional public schools tend to adopt a one-size-fits-none approach, while choice permits greater customization.

Third, and most important, there is no necessary tension between expanding school choice and competition and pursuing most other reforms. For example, if smaller class size is a desirable reform, we could facilitate that by allowing families to choose schools with smaller classes. The exit of some students from traditional public schools would certainly lower class sizes for the remaining students. Or if new technology is important to improving schools, then parents can choose schools that invest more in technology.

Choice is simply a method by which other reforms can occur. Whether we favor relying upon choice to facilitate other reforms or declare that choice is a "distraction" depends on whether we trust that centralized authorities are more likely to select the right reforms than decentralized schools that cater to choosing parents. Those arguing that choice is a "distraction" presume that they know the right way to design schools for all students. But do they? They believe they know how many teachers to hire, whom to hire as teachers, how to compensate them, what curriculum should be taught, how to assess progress, how much to invest in other staff, what technology to purchase, etc.

Moreover, those who view choice as a distraction from doing what they know works have to believe that they, or whoever the centralized authority is, will identify the best teachers, curriculum, pedagogy, etc., over time. They can't just pick the right school design, staffing, and content once; they have to make the right choices on behalf of others over and over as circumstances change and innovations occur.

In short, the "distraction" folks are believers in central planning. Why be distracted by messy markets when we can just tell businesses what they should be making (and in what quantities, by what method, etc.)? It is no secret that central planning hasn't worked out very well. It's nearly impossible for even the most benevolent central planner to know what works best for everybody and to keep updating what works best as new information is learned. And most central planners tend not to be so benevolent.

Education reformers are sometimes seduced by the allure of central planning without even realizing they are doing it. For example, Chester Finn and Michael Petrilli of the Fordham Institute have become enamored with national standards, curriculum, and assessments. Sol Stern of the Manhattan Institute has grown frustrated with the slow pace of improvement from school choice and wants us to take a great leap forward by imitating the curricular and pedagogical reforms instituted in Massachusetts. These reformers are not enemies of all markets in education: They still support choice (although sometimes weakly), but they think it is more important to focus on getting the "right" standards, curriculum, pedagogy, and assessments put into place.

But who is going to figure out what the right things are? Who is going to put them into place and keep them updated over time? These reformers implicitly assume that they or people who agree with them are likely to be in charge of deciding, implementing, and updating standards, curriculum, pedagogy, and assessments. I wish that could be true since, for the most part, I am personally inclined to favor the approaches advocated by Finn, Petrilli, and Stern. The problem is that the organized interests in education, including the teachers unions and their political allies, are much more likely to grab the reins of any central authority that decides these issues. Even if the unions and their allies do not dominate the process at the beginning, they are likely to seize control over time. And when they do control the centralized standards, curriculum, pedagogy, and assessment machinery that misguided reformers might build, they are unlikely to act so benevolently. They are likely to choose approaches that minimize burdens on their members even if those come at the expense of the educational interests of children.

The safest and best way to get quality curriculum, assessments, and pedagogy is to decentralize power through choice rather than to centralize power and pray that benevolent people with good taste and perfect judgment are forever in control.

Canard 7: Choice Is a Political Dead End

"Vouchers work," concedes Jay Mathews, the *Washington Post*'s education columnist, "but so what?" Mathews dismisses an effective reform strategy because he thinks it is a political dead end: "Efforts to create a national groundswell for vouchers have failed.... [D]espite a new crop of voucher-friendly governors, the prospects for a wave of pro-voucher votes across the country don't look good, at least not to me." The American Federation of Teachers concurs. "Vouchers are unpopular with the public, having been rejected – resoundingly and repeatedly – when they are on the ballot." And Sol Stern has bought this gloomy picture: "I focused on the dim prospects for expansion of voucher programs like Milwaukee's for the same reason that I wrote so hopefully about these programs in the past.... [T]he repeated failure to get voucher referenda passed in the states has been a blow to the movement. To say otherwise is to keep raising false hopes."

But since 2008, when Sol Stern wrote those

Choice is constrained because the vast majority of students continue to be assigned to schools based on where they live.

---

words, 15 private school choice programs were enacted or significantly expanded. A number of these programs target disabled students, while others provide private school scholarships to low-income students through tax-credit-supported organizations. And with seven new or significantly expanded programs already adopted during the current state legislative sessions, declaring the political death of private school choice is not just premature; it is downright false.

It is true that the total number of students attending private schools with government support still falls short of 200,000 out of the nearly 55 million school-age children. But new programs and more students are being added every year. In addition, once adopted, these programs develop their own political constituency that makes it nearly impossible to repeal. No private school choice program has been eliminated legislatively. Aside from a few adverse state court decisions, every choice victory is permanent, and every defeat is temporary.

More important, vouchers have made the world safe for charter schools. Charter school choice has grown dramatically over the past two decades. Twenty years ago, we had our first charter school; today, more than 5,400 charter schools serve about 1.7 million students. Political leaders from both political parties embrace the expansion of charter school choice, with Secretary of Education Arne Duncan making support for charter schools a factor in states receiving federal Race to the Top funds. Even the teachers unions have had to offer at least rhetorical support for charter schools, although they place so many conditions on their support that the only charter schools they really endorse are those that are unionized and virtually indistinguishable from traditional public schools.

None of this would have happened without the more threatening prospect of private school choice lurking out there. If the unions and their political allies were able to neutralize the voucher threat, they would have no more need to offer the compromise of supporting charters. So vouchers and tax credits have not just enabled nearly 200,000 students to attend private school with government support, but they have also made it possible for another 1.7 million students to attend charters. The growth and effectiveness of both kinds of choice is dependent on the continued expansion of private school choice.

Canard 8: We Already Have Enough School Choice

If we already have nearly 2 million students participating in tax-credit, voucher, or charter programs, and if we have millions more whose families choose where to live to gain access to a desired traditional public school, why do we need more school choice? We need more because existing choices are highly constrained, inequitably distributed, costly to exercise, and (most important) virtually never place serious pressure on traditional public schools to improve by hardly affecting their finances or jobs.

Choice is constrained because, as I noted above, the vast majority of students continue to be assigned to schools based on where they live. It is true that families can move to gain access to desired schools, but relocating is extremely costly and therefore not easily available to a large number of people. Moving because of schools doesn't just involve the expenses of a real estate transaction; it can also involve leaving jobs, friends, and families far behind. In addition, families may want to make different choices for different children or different choices for the same child over time. Moving is a highly inefficient way to provide choice.

But, most important, choice will only have broader effects when it can create significant competitive pressure on school systems. As discussed above, voucher, tax-credit, and charter choice has remained small enough in most places that these programs pose little competitive threat. Holding traditional public schools partially or entirely harmless to the loss of revenue as they lose students to these programs has further muted competitive pressures.

We need more school choice because we need to harness the same dynamic market forces that have facilitated progress in other domains of our lives to improve the abnormal, nonmarket domain of k-12 education. We are still in the very, very early stages of creating a productive k-12 education market. We should have confidence that expanding choice and competition in k-12 education will foster the same benefits that it does for us elsewhere. In the absence of convincing evidence to the contrary, we should believe that gravity works in this area just as it does in others.

The biggest obstacles to expanding choice and competition are the organized union interests and their political allies that directly benefit from the educational status quo. It is a bitter irony that this educational establishment is often assisted in its opposition to expanded choice and competition by elite families that already have reasonably good educational options for their own children. Wealthy families enjoy these options because they already have the resources to move to areas with desirable public schools or to pay the tuition at a private school. Taking their own privileges for granted, such families tend to be complacent about securing meaningful choice for others.

The organized power of the teachers unions combined with this complacency of wealthy elites makes expanding choice and competition a challenge. But the challenge is not insurmountable. Even wealthy families often find their choices too constrained for their liking and their schools academically inadequate. And maintaining this large, nonmarket enterprise in the midst of a society accustomed to choice and competition is incredibly hard to justify and maintain. It feels unnatural and requires constant rationalization.

The bottom line: If you want to improve primary and secondary education in America, you need to encourage school choice, not union control.

First American edition published in 2011 by Encounter Books,
an activity of Encounter for Culture and Education, Inc.,
a nonprofit, tax exempt corporation.
Encounter Books website address: www.encounterbooks.com

Manufactured in the United States and printed on
acid-free paper. The paper used in this publication meets
the minimum requirements of ANSI/NISO z39.48–1992
(R 1997) (*Permanence of Paper*).

FIRST AMERICAN EDITION

LIBRARY OF CONGRESS CATALOGING-IN-PUBLICATION DATA

Greene, Jay P., 1966–
Why America needs school choice / Jay P. Greene.
p. cm. — (Encounter broadsides)
ISBN-13: 978-1-59403-594-4 (pbk. : alk. paper)
ISBN-10: 1-59403-594-6 (pbk. : alk. paper)
1. School choice—United States. 2. Educational vouchers—
United States. I. Title.
LB1027.9.G74 2011
379.1 11—dc23
2011017578

10 9 8 7 6 5 4 3 2 1